Helen Chapman

Story illustrated by
Carl Pearce

In this story

 Adam

 Karl

 The harbour master

Tricky words

- against
- rough
- sloshed
- overboard
- straight
- moorings
- crouched
- despair
- groaned
- heave

Introduce these tricky words and help the reader when they come across them later!

Story starter

Karl and Adam were best friends. Karl's uncle owned a small fishing boat which was moored in a harbour.
One day, Karl's uncle asked the boys to tidy up the boat for him. Karl was working down in the hold while Adam was washing the deck. Then, disaster struck.

Danger Below

Karl and Adam were working hard.
Adam was washing the deck and
Karl was working down in the hold.
The sea, which had been as flat as a
pancake when the boys started working,
was now grey and choppy and the waves
were splashing against the boat.

"Have you nearly finished down there?" called Adam. "The sea is getting quite rough."

Karl climbed to the top of the ladder and looked up at the sky. There were dark clouds overhead. "We'd better finish quickly and get back on shore," he said.

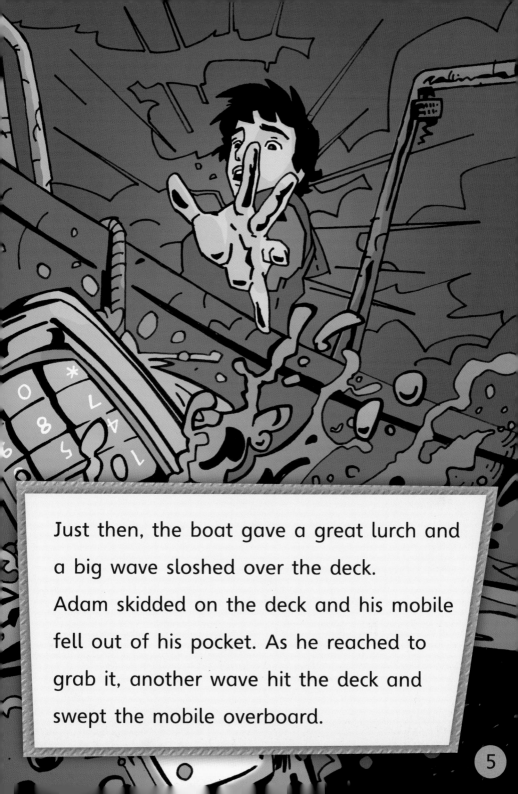

Just then, the boat gave a great lurch and a big wave sloshed over the deck. Adam skidded on the deck and his mobile fell out of his pocket. As he reached to grab it, another wave hit the deck and swept the mobile overboard.

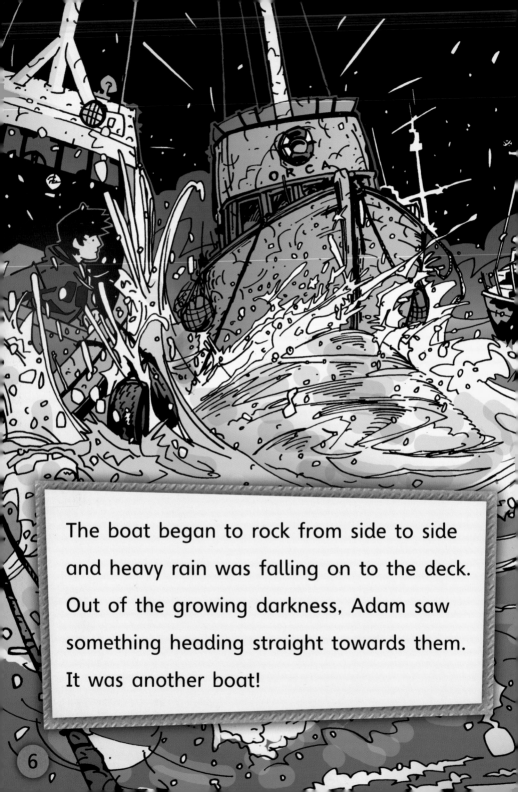

The boat began to rock from side to side and heavy rain was falling on to the deck. Out of the growing darkness, Adam saw something heading straight towards them. It was another boat!

"It must have slipped its moorings," thought Adam. But before he could shout a warning down to Karl, there was a loud crash and the sound of splitting wood. Then he heard Karl scream. Adam dashed over to the hold.

Karl was on the floor. His eyes were shut.
Beside him was a large spanner.

"It must have fallen from the shelf when the boat was hit," thought Adam.

Adam saw something else too – there was a hole in the side of the boat, and water was coming in.

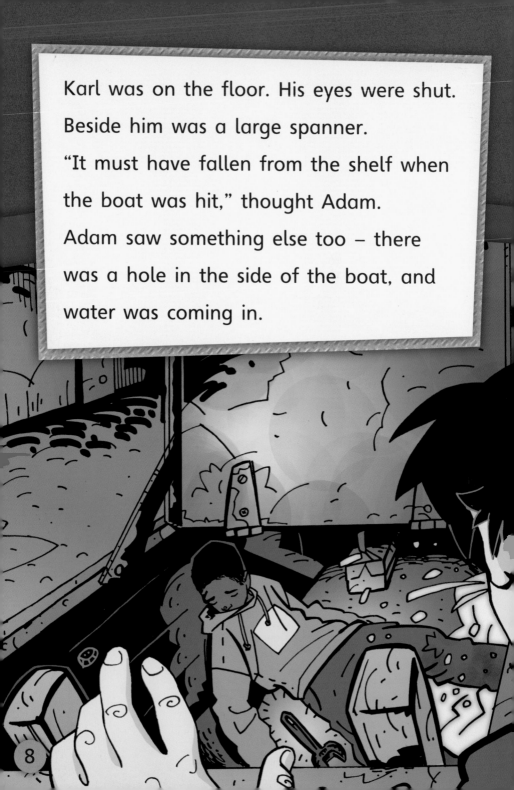

Adam rushed down the steps into the hold. He splashed across the floor and crouched down beside Karl.

"Are you all right, mate?" he asked.

But there was no answer.

"I need to get help," thought Adam, "and quickly!"

Adam felt in Karl's pocket for his mobile. He lifted it out and watched in despair as water trickled out of the handset.

Suddenly, there was a loud **CRACK** and sea water started pouring into the hold.

Adam felt a wave of panic sweep over him.
He knew he had to get Karl out before
the hold filled with water – the boat
would sink if much more water came in.
"If I don't move Karl soon, he'll drown,"
he thought.

Adam stared in horror at the hole in the side of the boat. Water was rushing in – there was no way he could stop it.

He dragged Karl's heavy body over to the ladder, but he knew that he wouldn't be able to carry him up the steps.

Just then, Karl opened his eyes. "What's going on?" he groaned.

"A spanner fell and hit you on the head," said Adam. "We need to get out of here." Karl looked at the water lapping around his knees. "You go," he said to Adam. "Get out while you can!"

"No way, mate," said Adam. "We
together! Hold on tight and I'll g
both up these steps."

"No, you go on," said Karl. "I'll n
make it. Get out or you'll drown t

"No chance," said Adam. "How wo
ever get back that fiver you owe r

Is Adam really
bothered about
the fiver?

Bit by bit, Adam made his way up the ladder. Karl did his best to help but he kept blacking out.

The water level was rising fast and Adam knew they were running out of time.

Then, with one final heave, he pulled them both out on to the deck.

A bright light shone in their eyes.

"You lads all right?" said a gruff voice.

They were looking into the friendly face of the harbour master.

"Adam saved my life," said Karl.

"Yeah, you owe me more than a fiver now!" said Adam.

Quiz

Text Detective

- Why couldn't Adam contact anyone for help?
- Do you think Adam was a good friend?

Word Detective

- **Phonic Focus:** Unstressed vowels
  Page 9: Which letters represent the unstressed vowel in 'answer'? (er)
- Page 3: What is the sea compared to?
- Page 16: Which adjective describes the harbour master's voice?

Super Speller

Read these words:

quite   something   working

Now try to spell them!

HA! HA! HA!

 What stories do sailors like to hear?

A Ferry tales!

17

Before Reading

Find out about

- How to cope in an emergency

Tricky words

- emergency
- survive
- flood
- building
- lightning
- pressure
- breath
- breathe

Introduce these tricky words and help the reader when they come across them later!

Text starter

There are lots of emergencies. You might be trapped in a flash flood or in a burning building, or even caught outside in a thunderstorm. Knowing what to do could save your life!

Emergency!

Do you know what to do in an emergency? Would you be able to survive a flash flood or get out of a burning building? Do you know how to make sure you're not struck by lightning? Read on to find out!

Emergency: Flash floods!

Can heavy rain kill you?

It can if there is a flash flood.

A flash flood can happen in a few minutes!

Heavy rain can quickly make rivers flood. Then the drains overflow and water pours out. It flows into towns, and floods buildings and roads.

People die in flash floods because they happen so quickly. When people try to cross a road covered in water, they can't tell how deep it is. Often, they fall and get swept away.

People also try to drive on flooded roads. The rushing water sweeps the car away and people can get trapped inside.

Trapped inside a sinking car

Here's what to do:

- Don't panic.
- A car will float for a short time, so open the door and get out.
- If you can't open the door, climb out of the window.
- If you can't open the window, try to break it or climb out through the sunroof, if there is one.

- If you can't open the door or window, wait. When the car is almost full of water, the pressure inside the car is the same as outside the car. This means you should be able to open the door.

- Take a big breath and hold it.

- Swim out.

Emergency: Fire!

Fires can spread very quickly.
A room can go up in flames in just a few minutes. Smoke from a fire can get into a room even if the door is shut. You cannot breathe in a smoke-filled room. Smoke is a killer!

Trapped inside a burning building

Here's what to do:

- Don't panic.
- Feel the door handle with the back of your hand.
- If the door handle is cold, open the door. Look for smoke or fire before going out. If you see smoke, crawl out.
- Get out of the building and then call for help.

- If the door handle is hot, don't open the door! A hot handle means the fire is just outside your room.
- Close any doors.
- Use your clothes to block any gaps around the door. This stops smoke getting into the room.

Dial 999 and ask for the fire service.

- If there is a phone, call the fire brigade.
- Go to a window and shout for help.
- Hang a sheet from the window, so people can see you.

Emergency: Lightning!

Can lightning kill you?

Yes!

Lightning is six times hotter than the Sun. If you can hear thunder, you're close enough to be hit by lightning.

When you see lightning, count the seconds until you hear thunder. If you can't count to more than 30, you could be in danger.

The best way not to get hit by lightning is to stay inside.

Wait 30 minutes after the last clap of thunder before you go back outside.

During a thunderstorm, do not use phones or computers, and unplug the TV.

Water conducts lightning, so this is not a good time to have a bath!

Trapped outside in a thunderstorm

Here's what to do:

- Don't panic.
- Find some shelter.
- Stay away from anything tall like trees and lamp-posts.
- Stay away from things made of metal.

- If you can't find shelter, stay low, but don't lie down on the ground.
- Crouch down, keep your feet together and stay on the balls of your feet. Keep your hands off the ground. If you feel your hair stand on end, drop into this position at once.

Quiz

Text Detective

- If you are trapped in a burning building, why should you feel the door handle before opening the door?
- Which do you think would be the scariest emergency?

Word Detective

- **Phonic Focus:** Unstressed vowels
  Page 28: Which letters represent the unstressed vowel in the word 'danger'? (er)
- Page 19: What do you notice about the first three sentences?
- Page 31: Find a word that means 'to bend down low'.

Super Speller

Read these words:

through   shout   minutes

Now try to spell them!

HA! **HA! HA!**

Q What do you call a sheep that has been struck by lightning?

A An electric blanket!